Dorothea Craemer

Hero of Faith

By Julie Stiegemeyer

Illustrated by John Martin

CONCORDIA PUBLISHING HOUSE · SAINT LOUIS

Edited by Rodney L. Rathmann
Assisted by Amanda G. Lansche

Manufactured in East Peoria, IL / 63692 / 160154

Table of Contents

Dorothea Craemer

It was 1845 on the rough seas of the Atlantic Ocean.

◆ ◆ ◆

chapter one
The Journey to a New Home

The boat swayed in the rhythm of the ocean as Dorothea Benthien cradled her sleeping son, Henry, in her lap. Her stomach was churning again with seasickness and worry, but Dorothea swallowed her fears and frustrations. The others needed her.

Henry's fever had flared up again. Smallpox ravaged many on board the *Caroline*. The ship had endured so many challenges during the last forty-five days.

Calendars marked the year 1845 as Dorothea cared for her five-year-old son, her friends, and the other passengers on board the ship traveling the rough Atlantic Ocean from Bremen, Germany to New York City. So many were sick and hurting. Dorothea worked tirelessly to help and comfort them.

Dorothea closed her eyes for a moment. So many days, so many troubles. First, they'd had to steer around Scotland due to high winds. Next, they had dodged icebergs, which were always a danger in the chilly Atlantic seas, especially in April when the spring thaw had barely begun. They'd even crashed into another boat, a trawler. The accident had not been serious enough to cause them to turn around, but each new problem caused more worry among the passengers.

Now, the smallpox sickness spread aboard the ship, disabling almost everyone. The illness caused red spots to appear on the skin along with fever and upset stomach. Just days before, a two-year-old child, Margaretha, had died from smallpox.

Dorothea breathed a prayer for the grieving parents and for all who were ill. Then she moved Henry gently to a blanket and attended to the others. She'd been traveling with a group of Lutherans moving from Germany to Fort Wayne, Indiana. She'd gotten acquainted with other Lutherans heading to America as well.

Dorothea prayed for God's help as she cared for those who were ill.

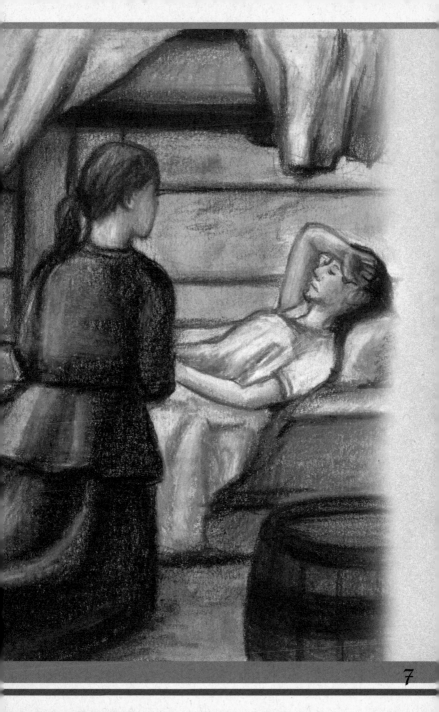

Pastor Craemer joined four couples in marriage on board the Caroline.

Among this group were four engaged couples, one married couple, two single men, and their pastor, Reverend Friedrich August Craemer (known as Pastor August Craemer), who was also single.

She'd learned from them, as they had lived together on this ship for nearly two months, that they were leaving their homes in Germany for the forests of Michigan in the United States. In their new home, Pastor Craemer would minister to the Lutherans in the area and reach out with God's love to the American Indians, the Chippewa. Pastor Craemer had explained that many German Lutherans had immigrated to Indiana, Ohio, Michigan, and the surrounding states, but had very few pastors to care for them.

"I volunteered to help," he had told her with
a grin during one of their many conversations,
"and help I shall. Teach and preach about Christ—
that's what I'll do."

Dorothea did not doubt him. He seemed
eager in his work and ready to carve out a new
home in Michigan. She admired him and found
herself spending more and more time with the
Michigan-bound Lutherans.

Pastor Craemer had begun his ministry even
before arriving in America. Shortly after boarding
the *Caroline*, he joined the four engaged couples
in marriage. Due to German laws, the couples had
not been able to marry before setting off on their

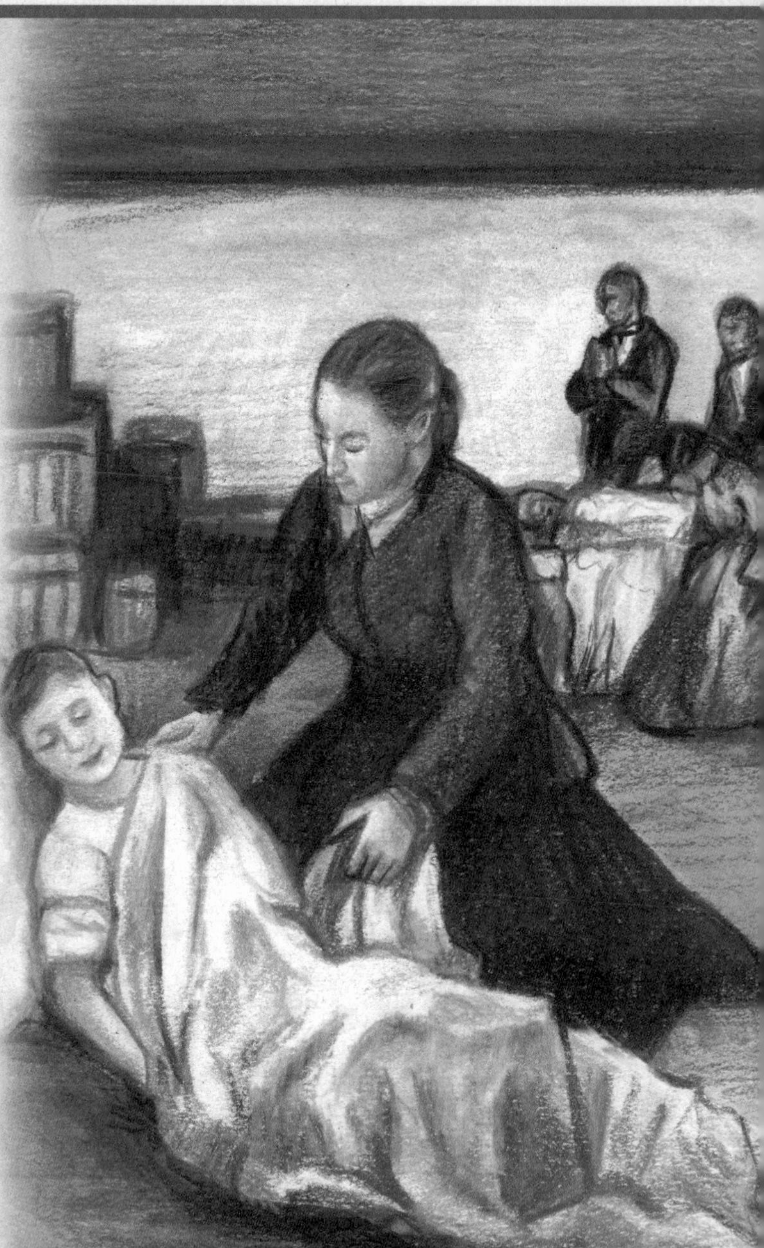

journey. But Pastor Craemer made quick work of that by conducting the marriage ceremonies shortly after the passengers were on board.

But their happiness was tempered by grief as the one couple among the group of the Michigan-bound Lutherans lost their young daughter to the smallpox epidemic. Their daughter was Margaretha Haspel, the little girl who had fallen asleep in Jesus when her little body could not withstand the demands of travel and disease.

Despite the risks, many groups of immigrants from Germany and other European countries voyaged to America. Between the years 1845 and 1860, millions of immigrants landed on American soil, seeking a better life. America was seen as a land of opportunity where there was plenty to eat, jobs to be had, and land on which to grow crops and build. And many of these large groups of immigrants did not have religious teachers and pastors to share God's gifts of forgiveness and grace with them.

So Pastor Craemer's group and others like his uprooted their lives back home and headed into the unknown. In their case, the unknown was the densely wooded forests of Michigan.

◆ ◆ ◆

chapter two
New Friendships, New Promises

More days passed, and Dorothea continued to nurse those suffering from sickness. But they were closer to their destination now. One afternoon, Dorothea went up on deck as the sea spray, salty and briny, splashed on her cheeks. She looked out at the ocean. She could see only water—the same blue-gray waves in all directions. Fifty days on board. How many more would pass until landfall?

Pastor Craemer walked up next to her.

"Miss Benthien," he said. "May I stand with you a moment?"

"Of course," she said.

"I have a question to ask you. I have noticed how you care for those who are ill." He paused and looked at Dorothea. "These are strangers you barely know, and yet you care for them like a loving mother."

Dorothea felt a bubble of curiosity. He'd noticed her?

"I wondered, Miss Benthien," he hesitated, "if you might be willing to work in this way in the wilds of Michigan?"

"In Michigan?" Dorothea was confused. "But I am going to Indiana."

"I know," he began, "but I am wondering if you might join us in Michigan instead."

Dorothea's brow furrowed. Michigan?

"Life would not be easy," he continued. "We have no homes, no buildings, only land."

Dorothea listened as he continued. "We will work among the Chippewa, whose language we do not know."

She nodded.

"I wonder," he said, "if you might be willing to work beside us knowing these things?"

Dorothea thought about it. She was strangely drawn to this man and his simple, straightforward speech.

"Well, actually," Dorothea said, almost surprising herself in agreement, "I would."

"Oh!" he stammered, "What I mean to say is, would you be willing to work—with me? By my side? As my wife?"

"Why, yes!" Dorothea said, blinking with surprise. "Yes, I would!"

"Then it shall be so," he said with a grin.

Dorothea smiled as she looked into his eyes.

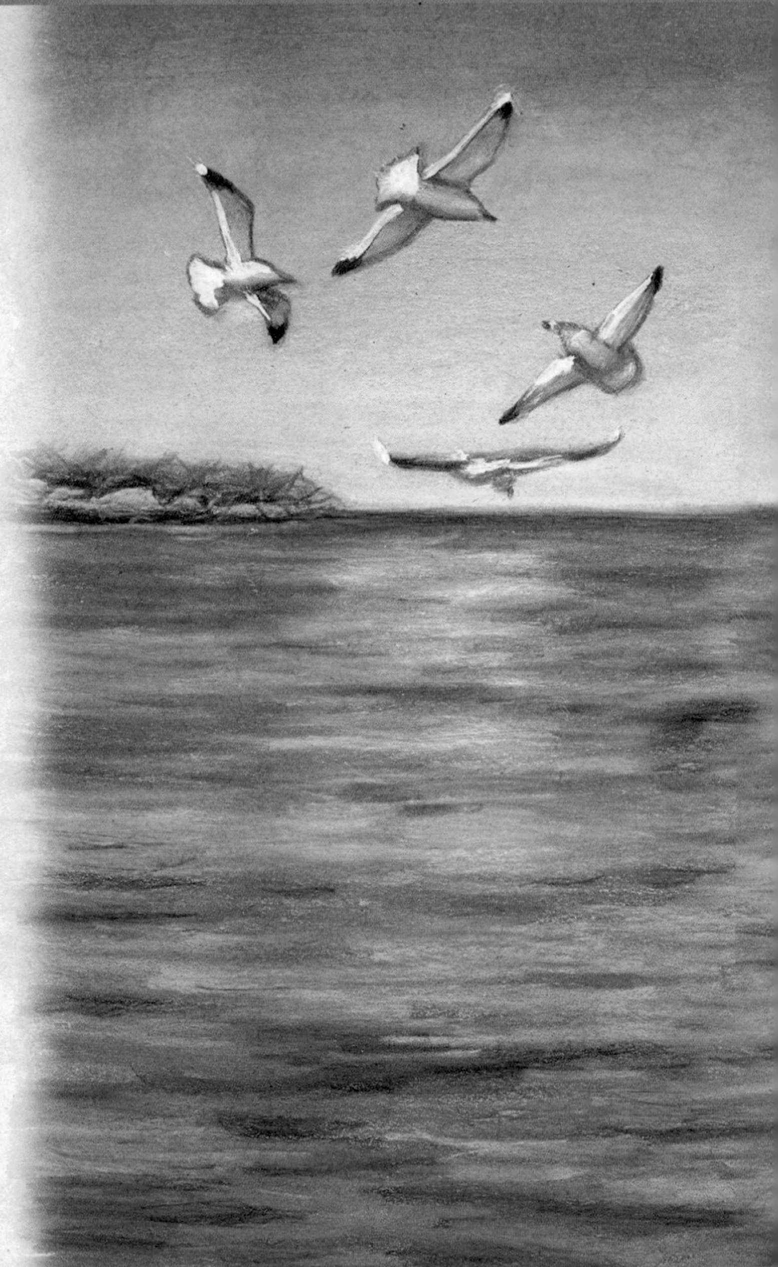

Amid all of the difficulties in this voyage, God had given her a wonderful blessing—a new family and a new home. Arm in arm, they went off together to tell the others. There was talk, though.

"She already has a son," some said.

"Yes, and where's the father?" others asked.

"Would she make a good pastor's wife?"

Though gossip accompanied their happy news, Dorothea, with Henry on one side and Pastor August Craemer on the other, ignored it. She was to be married and travel to a new home in Michigan.

It is unknown how Henry's biological father fits into her story. However, what is known is that Dorothea found no joy and fulfillment in the ways of the world. She was now a child of God through faith in Christ Jesus. Delighted and energized in the knowledge of Jesus as her Savior, Dorothea showed a willingness to serve in all situations, and her new fiancé, August Craemer, saw and treasured this quality in her.

America, at last!

◆ ◆ ◆
chapter three
Landfall!

Day 51 arrived on June 8, 1845, and with it came landfall. Smoke from fires all across New York City hung like a cloud above the settlement camps and buildings.

Dorothea clung to Pastor Craemer's arm as they waved at children who greeted them as their boat pulled into the harbor. America, at last!

On June 10, 1845, two days after their arrival in America, Dorothea entered the cool, dimly lit nave of Saint Matthew Lutheran Church in New York. "I am to be married," she whispered to herself, hardly believing that she would soon become the wife of Pastor August Craemer.

Words of promise spoken during the wedding ceremony hung between the two. God had brought them together. Now, they would take on the next part of their life together, trusting in God's grace and mercy.

And Henry was also there, watching and learning about God's love in action between his mother and his new stepfather. Soon, he would see God's love at work among American Indians in Michigan.

◆ ◆ ◆

chapter four

The Journey Continues

From New York City, the Lutheran immigrants boarded a train bound north to Albany and then west to Buffalo, New York. It would still be over twenty years before the First Transcontinental Railroad in America was completed. This railway would link the east coast with the west, from the Atlantic to the Pacific Ocean.

At this time in history, those moving west in search of land or opportunity usually traveled by covered wagon. As a matter of fact, just two years earlier, in 1843, a group of over one hundred covered wagons surged west on the Oregon Trail in what is known as the "Great

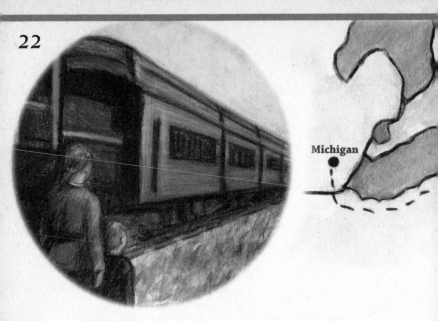

Michigan

Migration," as families left all that was familiar and placed their possessions in a rickety wagon to travel two thousand miles across the country. This was an important point in an annual tradition of groups making the trek west.

But the little band of Lutherans who had come all the way from Germany and across the Atlantic Ocean were now ready to travel the existing train lines to Albany, then Buffalo, and eventually to the heart of Michigan.

Dorothea, now Mrs. August Craemer, took Henry by the hand as they found seats on the last car of the train.

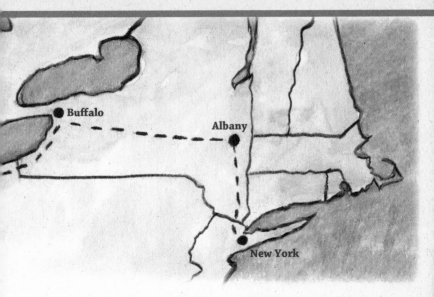

"Did you get a good look at the locomotive, Mama?" Henry asked after they had taken their seats.

"Yes, dear, I saw it—and now I can hear and feel it as well," Dorothea said. As the train screeched forward, they felt beneath them the increasing cadence of metal wheels rolling along on the rails of the track.

Travel in 1845 was difficult, tiring, and long. Already, the group had journeyed for nearly two months, and the trip was far from over. They had not even arrived in Michigan yet. Once they did, their work would have just begun. The land where they were going to live was densely wooded and sparsely inhabited. In order to make a home in Michigan, they would have to clear some of the trees and then build huts or cabins for their new homes.

◆ ◆ ◆

chapter five
Train Wreck!

In the warmth of that mid-June day, the train continued chugging its way across the state of New York. Henry had fallen asleep, resting his head on Dorothea's lap. Dorothea and her new husband, Pastor Craemer, were discussing the supplies they would need before heading into the wilderness.

"First," he began, "I'll go ahead with the other men, and we'll begin clearing the land and building a new home."

"Where will Henry and I go?"

"You'll stay with the other women in the nearby town of Saginaw. That way, I'll have time to build you a home." He took her hand.

Dorothea smiled. She'd been on her own for so long. It felt odd yet comforting to be cared for in this way.

"We could gather supplies," Dorothea suggested. "And perhaps learn about local plants and food—and get used to American ways."

The train bumped along the tracks in the background as they planned their future together.

Then—suddenly—there came a deafening noise of metal upon metal as the wheels screeched along the tracks! The sudden stopping of the train threw passengers forward. People tumbled off their seats.

"Mama!" Henry cried. He had been tossed to the floor like a doll, and Dorothea landed nearly on top of him. She grabbed his little body and hugged him to herself.

What was happening?

And then came the impact: CRASH!

The train rocked forward suddenly, whip-lashing passengers already on the floor of the car. People were screaming. Everything was in chaos.

They'd had a head-on collision with another train.

Minutes passed, dust settled, and the screams were replaced with moans as people began to get up from the places where they'd been thrown. Dorothea, Henry, and the others in their car inspected themselves and their belongings, thanking God that no one was seriously injured. There were a few scrapes and bruises, but their car was the last on the train, so they had escaped the brunt of the crash.

"Are you okay?" Dorothea asked Henry. He nodded, but had a frightened look in his eyes. They got off the train as Pastor Craemer rushed forward to minister to the badly injured and dying. Dorothea longed to help too, but Henry was frightened.

"It's okay, lamb," she said. "We're safe now." She whispered a prayer to God for the safety of those injured.

This collision was yet another in the long line of difficulties they faced while traveling in 1845.

After their tumultuous journey by ship, train, and boat, they finally arrived in Saginaw, Michigan, on July 10, 1845. Here, the men and women parted ways. The men went ahead to accomplish the enormous task of clearing the land and beginning to build a structure for shelter.

Dorothea, along with the other women and Henry, stayed behind. Two months later, the men sent word that they had cleared some land and had begun work on building two huts, one for communal use and one for the parsonage.

And into the unknown, with faith and prayer, Dorothea went again.

◆ ◆ ◆

chapter six
A New Home

Time passed quickly during the early months at their new home. Dorothea found life here much different than her native Germany. Mosquitoes buzzed and bit. The heat and humidity felt like a heavy cloud. Dirt encrusted everything—nearly all of her clothing— and Dorothea simply could not seem to wash it out in the chilly waters of the nearby creek. But this morning, she tried yet again.

She was wringing out Henry's linen tunic, her hands already red and raw from the cold water of the creek. She shook out the tunic once more and gathered up the rest of her wet and heavy laundry. She walked up the pathway to the two huts in the clearing.

"Good morning!" she called to Lorenz and Martin, two of the men in their group. They were fitting a log into place in the cabin they were building next to the huts. The wall was already about five feet high. Soon, they'd be able to put on the roof—hopefully, they would finish before winter.

The settlement was built near the Cass River in the densely wooded area of eastern Michigan. Although the weather was hot and uncomfortable for the pioneers, their garden thrived in the Michigan summer.

They settled near the Cass River in a densely wooded area.

In addition to the cooking, cleaning, mending, sewing, and washing, Dorothea and the others also tended the garden. Already they were harvesting some vegetables—cabbage, onions, parsnips, and turnips.

Dorothea hung the laundry outside on the line near the hut, which was built with two purposes. It was the church as well as the parsonage where the pastor and his family lived. The rest of the group lived in the communal hut.

"Guten tag!" a familiar voice called out. "Good day!" It was Pastor Craemer, walking into the clearing near the huts.

"August!" Dorothea called; she set her laundry

down to greet her husband.

The others gathered around too, and Pastor Craemer scooped Henry up and spun him around.

"How was your journey?" Dorothea asked.

"Unlike last week, the canoe did not tip over while we were crossing the lake!" he said with laughter. "I had moose stew for supper last night and slept in a wigwam, which is really a snug little house, not unlike our own!"

He went over to look at the progress on the log cabin, patting the solid log wall. "Soon, we'll be able to worship here in a more permanent home."

◆ ◆ ◆

chapter seven

A Christmas to Remember

The last of the autumn leaves swirled into a mini tornado as the chilly wind blew. The first snow had fallen the week before but had quickly melted on still soft and warm ground. Winter had only just begun.

"Hurry, Mama!" Henry zipped along the trail from the creek, rushing ahead of Dorothea. The afternoon sun was already fading in the west, though it was not quite dinnertime. They had made one more trip to the creek to fetch water.

Night was falling quickly. As they turned around the last bend on the path, Dorothea saw her husband lighting a candle in the log cabin. They'd punched in the last nail that afternoon. It was Christmas Eve 1845, and their little church in the Michigan wilderness was completed. A desk served as the pastor's pulpit. A box at the front of church had been transformed into an altar, which held the cup and plate that would be used for Holy Communion.

Christmas Eve 1845,
their little church in the
Michigan wilderness was complete.

And on the next morning, a tiny congregation in the woods sang praise to the baby born in Bethlehem on that Christmas long, long ago. As they worshiped on that Christmas morning, Dorothea turned to Henry on her one side and her husband on the other. Life was a struggle, but it was a joy-filled struggle with faith in God. She thought back to all of their adventures and trials of the last few months, whispered a prayer of thanksgiving, and joined in the verse: "From heav'n above to earth I come!"

The following Christmas,
Pastor Craemer baptized
several of the Chippewa children.

38

Dorothea and Henry welcome the Chippewa children into their home.

chapter eight
"Mutter"

Dorothea looked around their little hut as she rinsed the shiny black hair of the girl they called Anna. Children from one of the Chippewa villages swarmed around her. It was warm inside the cozy but very small hut. She spotted Henry playing a game with a Chippewa boy about his size. They mainly gestured to each other to communicate, but Henry understood more and more of the Ojibwa language every day.

"Mutter," said another of the little girls. "Mama!" Maria was pulling on her skirts. "Mutter!" she repeated. The children often called her "Mama" or "Mutter" when she cared for them.

"Yes, I see you," Dorothea said as she dried Anna's hair. "You are next."

The wide, happy eyes of Maria looked up sweetly. She was waiting patiently, but it was difficult.

Maria hopped up on the little stool and bent over the basin of water, so trusting and hopeful. Dorothea soaped and rinsed her hair. Then, Maria, with a flash of a smile, whipped her head around and shook like a wet dog.

"All dry!" she said, giggling as everyone complained.

"Oh, silly Maria," Dorothea wiped the water off her face and hugged the little rascal. "As soon as you are dry, I will tell you children a story about Jesus from the Bible."

While Dorothea and Henry welcomed the Chippewa children into their home, Pastor Craemer preached and taught in villages near their settlement. The Chippewa lived in small groups and used the bark from birch trees as the "skin" for their wigwams. Every spring, they would strip a thin layer of bark off of a birch tree and sew the pieces carefully together.

Then, they would stretch a tentlike roof between willow branches and construct a new home. They feasted on berries native to the Michigan woods as well as fish, moose, and rabbit. They also grew their own corn.

To bring the Good News to the Chippewa, Pastor Craemer traveled mostly by foot. At times, though, he was able to get a ride in a canoe along the river or across one of the lakes. Pastor Craemer went from village to village to tell the Bible's message of hope and salvation for all through Christ. His work yielded friendships as well as cooperation between the new immigrants and the natives of the land.

Pastor Craemer preached and taught in villages near their settlement.

Epilogue

Dorothea lived out her remaining years alongside her husband as he continued his work of preaching and teaching. More German immigrants joined their band of believers in Michigan, and the town soon grew into a larger settlement as more homes and log cabins were added to the original camp from 1845.

In time, the people came to love Dorothea, saying she was the best pastor's wife they could have and that God surely led Pastor Craemer to her on the *Caroline*. Through their work among the Chippewa, God brought many souls to faith in Jesus Christ. Only a few months after setting foot in Michigan, Pastor Craemer baptized several of the Chippewa children. Dorothea cared for many of these children in her home, teaching them about Jesus and caring for them like a loving mother.

After a few years in Michigan, the Craemer family moved to Dorothea's original American destination, Fort Wayne, Indiana, where Pastor Craemer became the president of the seminary located there and trained students to become pastors. While living in Fort Wayne, Dorothea was, of course, busy. She ran the school's commissary, which was much like a cafeteria. So again, like a mother (or "mutter"), she provided those around her with their

basic needs of food and home. In addition to Henry, she
and Pastor Craemer had eight more children. She truly
was a blessed "mutter"!

*As an adult, Henry helped
bring the Good News to
other Chippewa.*

Interestingly, although Henry did not become a
pastor like his stepfather, he did continue to live and
work among the Chippewa. His childhood experiences
among these native people taught him their language.
When he was still a young man, Henry traveled west to

help missionaries learn the Chippewa language so that they might bring the Good News of salvation in Christ to the Chippewa living in that region. He also translated portions of God's Word (presumably) from German to the Chippewa language in order to bring God's message of hope to them.

The mission in the forests of Michigan thrived in the years after its humble beginnings. Soon, the settlement along the river where the Craemers first lived became known as Frankenmuth. Frankenmuth grew to become home to many more people in the coming years, and the congregation established there became one of the founding churches of The Lutheran Church—Missouri Synod. The congregation thrives today.

Dorothea died on November 11, 1884, while kneeling at her bedside in prayer. This seems fitting, for Dorothea's life was filled with prayer as she walked through life with faith and trust in her Savior, Jesus. She will be long remembered as a hero of faith—one of the bold and courageous pioneers who, trusting in Jesus, set out from Germany with her unknown future in God's hands. Along the way, she embraced those around her with love and affection, always kept an attitude of prayer, and in so doing, came to know God's gift of contentment.

Dorothea found contentment knowing Jesus as her Savior.

Timeline of Events
during Dorothea Craemer's Life

1818   Dorothea Benthien is born.

1819   Spain cedes Florida to the United States.

1825   Erie Canal opens.

1845   Dorothea and Friedrich August Craemer met on a ship going to America; they marry upon landing in New York City.

1846   Neptune discovered.

1847   The Lutheran Church—Missouri Synod begins.

1857   Dred Scott decision in U.S. Supreme Court.

1860   Lincoln elected president of the United States.

1869   Cincinnati Red Stockings established (first Major League Baseball team).

1876   Alexander Graham Bell invents the telephone.

1884   Dorothea Craemer dies.

Author's Note

My great-grandmother, Katherine Schlegel Hartman, was born in 1876 aboard a ship much like Dorothea's as she and her family voyaged from Europe to New York City. I recently found the ship's manifest with her mother's and father's names listed as well as sisters and brothers and one "Catharina, 13 days child, born at sea" written in careful longhand. Being a mother myself, I wonder at my great-great-grandmother who boarded an immigrant ship knowing her preborn child could be born—or lost—at sea.

My ancestors were Volga Germans, those of German ancestry who resettled in Russia after leaving their homeland to find food and work. Then, they resettled in America, traveling across the country to Kansas. They carved out a new place for themselves through the life and times God gave them in the heartland of America.

That is why, at least in part, Dorothea's story of drama and courage is so meaningful to me. Here is this Lutheran woman seeking a new life and finding God's treasures and gifts along every unknown turn, much like my ancestors who traveled to a distant land to find hope.

Dorothea's story also resonates with me because she is a Lutheran pastor's wife, as I am. And Sunday after Sunday, as my husband preaches to the people in our congregation and community, I think that maybe, in a small way, I am helping to pass along the legacy of our early Lutheran sisters such as Dorothea, who served alongside her husband and cared for those around her.